CALLING

The Calling

SELECTED POEMS BY

DOROTHEA NEALE

True North Press

True North Press

ISBN: 979-8-218-99422-8

Cover Art © 2025 lin boulay. All rights reserved - used with permission.
Cover design: Magda Carrero-Zerilli
Content edits: Ava Rayne Zerilli
Production Management: Leith I. ter Meulen

PRINTED IN THE UNITED STATES OF AMERICA

Dedicated to Poets Past, Present, and Future

"With the magic carpet of poetry, we can explore facets of our historical past or travel wherever it may take us. Yet, how many inspired ideas and splendid words that might become immortal are like 'words written on the wind' if they remain hidden away in a poet's heart or notebook, unshared? Within the pages of a book, the words can be read and re-read, available as a constant and fulfilling part of our lives, to become part of the lasting treasure of poetry. "
Dorothea Neale

Table of Contents

Introduction to Poetry

When I was a child and went to bed,
Out of some book my mother read
Fairy tale, legend and history, Saying and fable and poetry.

Every night before I would sleep,
With song and verse there was tryst to keep,
And as she spoke, before my mind's eye
People and places paraded by.

Of all she might read that I loved best,
It was poetry led all the rest;
In music and meaning her words flowed along,
Bringing me story and picture and song.

—〰—

Gems

The little old gilded-tiled carved jewel
chest from the bottom of her trunk.
She opened it to look again at the contents.
She looked at it. She sighed. Old gold.
Old memories, old dreams, old reactions.

It was worth an ounce.

She tucked several pieces
of a letter carefully folded
into the envelope they would not encumber
that morning. She had decided that
a grief that seemed to be separated hand
wrought.

She hesitated a moment, then
quickly before she could change her mind,
she slipped it into the envelope and sealed the flap.

Heavily she put on her coat and hat.

—⟨∿⟩—

Words

Poets speak with jeweled words,
Sweeter than songs of singing birds.

Gossips deal with words barbed
That dig sharp words that will not heal.

Like golden bells a saint's voice rings,
Words that uplift like golden wings.

Mothers with words make lullaby,
Healing the throat, stilling the cry.

With lovers each word a caress
To hold a world of happiness.

Words can be so many things:
Jewels & swords & shining wings.

—◦∿◦—

Needs

I need the city, I need the sea;
I need the countryside's green;
I need a garden spot to stay,
And paths to wander up and down.

I need the dawn, the sun-bright day;
I need the dusk, the velvet night;
I need the ever-changing moon,
And stars with steady jewels' light.

At times I need to be alone;
Again, to mingle with the throng;
I need to dance, I need to sing,
I need the silence, and a song.

Glow

I'd rather be alone
With my thoughts of you;
Walking 'neath a starry space,
With dreams and memories true.

I slip from crowd and lighted rooms,
Into the friendly night;
And there alone I somehow find
A better light.

The glow of friendship warm and true,
Between your soul and mine,
Though storms may come and clouds may mar,
Will stand unshaken, sublime.

———✦———

Words II

A cruel word is a poisoned dart,
That tears and rends the tender part,
And makes a wound within the heart.

A kind word like a bird that sings,
In sound or silence an echo rings,
As music, joy and warmth it brings.

An ugly word has an evil smell,
Of spoiled things the odors tell,
That no deodorant can quell.

While a lovely word is like a flower,
Whose fragrance sweetens every hour,
And makes the mind a garden bower.

A false word is like a fog;
Treacherous, filled with smoke and smog;
Or in a swamp, a broken, hollow log.

While a true word is like a rock,
That holds firm when falsehoods flock,
Sturdy, that nothing can stir or mock.

A word is like a dagger sharp and strong,
Or a word is as lilting and sweet as a song.
Both stay in the heart and echo long.

—⁓—

Talisman

If feigned indifference
Would bring you to my feet
And make you wholly mine,
I still could not pretend
To what I cannot feel.

I have not strength to dim my love,
Or cloud its brightness.
The puny thing that some call pride
Is but a doll of wax within its glow;
I have not strength for that.

But I have strength to let you go;
To see, dear one, the world
Has other things for you.
By not one hair's breadth would I
Swerve your need to mine.

But only let my love mean this to you:
A talisman against all hurt or harm,
A shining light when night must come.

—◈—

A Book

He ate and drank the precious words,
His spirit grew robust;
He knew no more that he was poor,
And that his frame was dust.

He danced along the dingy days,
And this bequest of wings,
Was but a book. What liberty
A loosened spirit brings!

———∽∽∼———

A Day

There was a summer day we spent
In Maryland; through wooded pathways went
Until we found a rocky way,
And climbing it, surprised the bay,
And oh, the bay was blue;
We stood awhile to watch the view,

The Chesapeake was stretched out wide,
But we could see the other side,
Cottages, piers, an anchored boat,
And on the water, white sails afloat
To match clouds in the sky;

We rested there, took time to lie
Stretched in the sun, then from our ledge
We clambered down to water's edge
Through bush and sand our way we made;
The sun and wind on water played,
The world was sun and bay and blue,

White clouds and white sails drifting through;

Then from my shoes I shook out sand,
And sat to draw a circle with one hand,
And found my fingers touch a tiny shell
That I have still; we heard the bell
Of near-by buoy ring warning clear,
To passing ship to venture not too near
A hidden shoal; a freighter went past,

An hour's ride to reach the port at last;
To crowded, sun-swept beaches down the bay,

A steamer made its last trip of the day;
We saw the lowering sun, could not but know
Reluctantly, that it was time to go;

We left, but once again we turned,
The reddening sky a glittering pathway burned
Across the bay, while waters grayed;
Silver in changing light the ripples played;

And so remains a vision of the day,
We unexpected came, and found the bay.

———⁓⁓⁓———

Hill Dreams

Walking makes me dream of hills,
Cascades where crystal water spills;
Stones across a laughing brook,
Vistas with every turn and look,
Framed with tree trunks, boughs arching high
Far hills grey-blue against blue sky.

Walking takes me back again
To the days that I knew when
From a hill-encircled town—
I wandered, pathways up and down,
From early spring until late in fall
Following my wild birds' call.

Walking till the sun, in heat
Weathered as they seemed in fleet,
Venturing up stone-rough way
Or in a ghetto refuge stay—
Knowing thus a green retreat
Picking wildflowers at my feet.

Though I walk on city streets,
Yet I hear the mountain song;
Waters dance, wild birds call
As I move among the throng.
And somehow strangely am awake,
Of flowers' sweet fragrant air,
While the clouds that rise fill skies
Violet grey hills against the sky,

The columns were softly white in the deepening twilight
And softly white the stars in the dusky sky;

The rain washed air was fragrant with late spring;
The warm earth, the grasses, the olive trees,
For the sacred grove that lay before the temple
Was in flower and new leaf; their fragrance
Was like an offering before the temple,

Even as later would be the fruit;
Flower, fragrance, fruit, all in its own time of unfolding;

There among the columns I waited for my Beloved;
The columns waited with me; the trees waited;
And the stars waited with me;
The path, trod by countless feet for many centuries,
The path waited, too, for no other footsteps
Were as your footsteps; and all the night
Was hushed with expectancy.

No leaf fell from the trees, no dust stirred upon the path;
Even the stars seemed not to move;
And I neither moved nor spoke,
But listened with the greatest intensity,
For that sound that would herald your coming,
Your feet upon the beaten path;
In the distance the sound of your steps;
Closer they came and swiftly;

I moved forward, breathless and eager for your coming,
My heart beating as accompaniment to your approach;

You were there! I went into the circle of your arms,
And you held me as though you would never let me go;
(As if I would go, or in going ever fail to return)
My right hand fingered your hair, touching your curls
Until I felt the golden circlet upon your brow,
And you held me so close, I could feel the muscles
Rippling beneath your girdled tunic; and you smiled.
And our hearts together chimed a song of love,

And the little leaves fluttered and whispered
In all the trees, and the winds stirred among them,
Caressingly, shaking forth their fragrance;
Stars twinkled and went upon their accustomed way,
Alive and was music.

—⁊⁊⁊—

The autumn colors fade.
Lost is the season's gold."

Winds tear at near-bare branches,
And nights turn cold.
The grapes have all been weighed;
Juice crushed for jelly or wine;
Only the pumpkin now remains upon the vine.

The first frost has come,
Put the last fall flowers to sleep,
But in the cellar is treasure,
Apples for winter's keep.

The nuts have been gathered,
From trees that yield best;
Now earth is sombre, still,
All nature keyed for rest.
How it is night upon the hill,
And stars in all their wonderful
Jeweled light into the nearby lake,
Where the star reflections make

A small piece of mirrored sky.
We look into the valley, try
To tell from lights we see
Whether they come from spots we know;
Watch them go out one by one
Until the last faint light is done.

Across the valley far hills lie
Like heaped up clouds against the sky.
Here we shall sleep on hill top bed,
Where the ground is thickly spread
With needles from a fragrant pine,
And think of stars more brightly shine
Than those above us.

—✺—

Pulse of Nature

Every season has its part,
As the endless rhythms flow
In the beat of Nature's heart.

Roots awake with spring and start
The rising sap that leaf may grow;
Every season has its part.

Summer is a flower mart,
Blossom fragrant breezes blow
In the beat of Nature's heart.

Autumn comes, fulfills the chart,
With reaped harvest it can show
Every season has its part.

Piercing winds of winter dart,
Yet earth knows coverlet of snow,
In the beat of Nature's heart.

Each cycle a recurring start,
Seeds must fall to newly sow;
Every season has its part,
In the beat of Nature's heart.

—⁓—

Moon Chimes

The moon is a golden bell.
A Bell.
The sound of a bell is a haunting sound,
And it hammers at the heart;
With all the joys and all the fears,
Of which bells were ever a part.

—⁓—

Your Tree of Good

May every bell and every ball
Symbolize a wish come true;
And every ball and every bell
Bring a hope fulfilled to you—

May every ball with color bright
Shine to make your world come right,
And every bell to soundly ring
The best of all life's gifts to bring
Shine with color, ring with song

Make of life a harmony;
The silver angel ever sings
Her guardian song of melody.

—⁓—

Response to Music

Music is like a rising sea,
With sweeping tides of melody,
To engulf us in harmony.

Music is like a wind to blow,
Softly at first, then rising slow
Till its wide sweep is all we know—

Music might be a growing light
To break the silence, as the night
Is broken by the dawn, rose-bright.

Slowly at first, till rising sound,
Seems to lift us from the ground,
While soul and senses start to pound.

Till we are caught within its spell,
As chord and cadence strike and swell,
And, in a world, all music dwell.

Then slower, fainter, come the beats,
While the wealth of sound retreats,
Till memory's ears alone repeats.

Yet silence now is not the same,
Nor do our senses seem quite tame,
While darkness glows with hidden flame.

Long shall these threads of melody,
And all the throb of harmony,
Resound within the memory.

———∿∿∿———

Harvest

Wheat tied up in golden sheaves;
Autumn brings both fruit and seed.

Russet rich colors from tree to weed,
Golden bright the pattern weaves;
Beauty and bread to meet man's need.

The season's changes ever speed;
Fruit turns to wine but no one grieves,
Autumn brings both fruit and seed.

Time's nimble footsteps onward lead,
Wind-blown are seeds and gold-brown leaves;
Beauty and bread to meet man's need.

Riches to reward the deed,
Who plants the seed, harvest receives;
Autumn brings both fruit and seed,
Beauty and bread to meet man's need.

—⁓⁓—

Gifts

You gave me a small flower,
And with it a smile;
And no doubt you thought
I kept each but brief while.

But the white fragrant flower,
If you happened to look
You would find between pages
Of a favorite book.

While the smile that you gave,
If you could but see,
Is held deep in my heart,
In lasting memory.

———

Dancing Light

There are ripples on the river,
And the sunlight dancing there;
The wind is in the willows,
And there's magic in the air.

The wind is telling stories,
And the dew-filled earth so fair
Is a song of wind and sunlight.

Wavering shadows on the grass,
And all the fingers of the trees
Strum music as they pass
Among the rippled rivers
Until all the light

Is filled with dancing light!

There are ripples on the river,
And the sunlight dancing there;
The wind is in the willows,
And there's magic in the air.

The wind is telling stories,
And the dew-filled earth so fair
Is a song of wind and sunlight.

Wavering shadows on the grass,
And all the fingers of the trees
Strum music as they pass
Among the rippled rivers
Until all the light
Is filled with dancing light!

———〰〰———

Alchemy

Oh, turn your tears to crystal,
Of silver make your pain,
You'll find there in a hidden strength,
Sorrow can yield its gain.

Forge them all to gleaming jewels,
And lovely filagree,
However heavy they may lay,
Yet wear them gracefully.

Singing Heart

Laughter can hide and heal the hurt
That tears could never ease;
And between the heart that sighs,
And between the heart that sings,
There's that that changes tragedy
To triumph on its wings.

———⟊⟊⟊———

A Rainy Day

Starting mistily at dawn,
The rain came down all day,
Dimming all the distances
And turning them to gray.

The rain started so lightly,
One looked twice to make sure,
But after a pause gained momentum
And came with a real downpour.

With increase of tone and tempo,
The winds joined forces to blow;
Trees seemed like ships in a tempest,
Scarce knowing which way to go.

Passengers battling the street,
Struggled quite in vain,
Hats lost, umbrellas inside out
Between the wind and rain.

Mid-afternoon the winds went down,
Wet tree branches stood secure;
Huddled birds shook out their wings,
Glad they could endure.

Rains stopped, patches of sky appeared,
A shaft of light shot out,
From the hidden sun whose gleam,
Gold flecked the scattered clouds about.

Suddenly across the sky,
A rainbow arched its way;
Symbol of hope and glory
For the end of a rainy day.

The rains of spring fell lightly
Over the earth in a soft shower
Gently falling on the boughs
Answering each leaf and flower.

Luxurious rains of summer
Lingered long to fill
The rivers, lakes well filled
Refreshed every field and hill.

The mournful rains of autumn
Drenched the leaves as they fell.
While rains of winter
Turn to hail & sleet & snow

Suddenly across the sky,
A rainbow arched its way;
Symbol of hope and glory
For the end of a snowy day.

*"The fears are golden in the sun
and heavy on the boughs."*

—◦◦◦—

One Thought

One clear, silver star
Lights up the dim blueness
Of the deepening twilight;
And one white and fragrant water-lily
Stars the darkening garden pool
Within the garden;

One thought flowers
In my heart,
My thought of you, and stars
The lonesome night with wonder.

Fragrance and light enfold me tenderly,
Within the twilight of my need for you.

———✦———

You Are Not Here

Night pains me with its beauty
    Because you are not here;
The trees are singing love songs,
    The sky is bending near.

The hours are filled with sweetness
    In a world made just for dreams,
The hours are hushed, expectant,
    As the moon showers silver dreams.

All the world is sweet enchantment,
    A night made for us, my dear,
But its beauty is but heartbreak
    Because you are not here.

More Than Lonesome

I'm more than lonesome for you tonight.
The soft winds sigh and the moon is white;
The moon is white and the soft winds call,
And shadows lie on the garden wall.

Even the stars are lonesome it seems,
Scattered and pale: while a white moon gleams
On an empty world with its lack of you,
And hours are long as the night wears through.

Do not say you love me yet,
Although your love would be
Like sweet enchantment through my blood,
And hours of ecstasy.

Do not say you love,
Though love has come so soon,
I would not miss the dawning,
For sake of brightest noon.

Love Me Thus

Love me fiercely,
As waves beating upon the sand,
The sun drinking up the sea,
Wind having its way with a tree;
Stir me as the wind
Stirs the grasses upon the plain:
Sweep upon me like a river
Moving inexorably to sea.

Love me tenderly,-
Gently as the petal of a flower
Falls to earth, as caressingly,
As a blossom holds a drop of dew;
As softly as the sun warms the earth
And stirs the sleeping roots
To reach upward for embrace;
As caressingly as a musician
Draws a love song from his instrument.

Love me completely,-
Possess me, make me utterly yours,
Drink me down like a glass of rare wine;
Claim me as wind claims a cloud,
Flames turning wood into flames;
Hold me as the sun holds a planet
Inescapably within its orbit;
Let me sink as your love
Drown me in its depths,
Sweep me into the vortex
Of your desire for me,

To complete and joyful surrender.
There is such happiness as I
see that I knew not
With gladness ever present
That I never dreamed or knew
now that I have you.

Life takes on a different meaning
Since you came along.
Such wealth of tenderness is gift
My days are filled with song.

—◆—

Reflections

Light on water is a lovely thing,
Moonlit fountains as they softly fling
Their silver spray on darkened pool below;
Mistily shining rain in yellowed glow
Centered from lamps in city streets at night,
Where wet streets darkly shine from

We shall go along tonight
Sometimes a shadowed path
in soft lights leads us.
The magic is the air
and our joy is the goal.

I shall not find delight
Where tall shadow flows;
And love shall be my guide.

—◈—

Moon Songs

The moon is a silver spider
That weaves a web of light
To catch in a silver cobweb,
All that strolls the night.

—∿∿—

Moon Fruit

The moon is a rich golden fruit
Hung on the tree of night,
And every night the waning moon
Steps up to take a bite,
Until her growing sister moon
Comes by and would repair
And adds the gold back
Bit by bit
Till all of it is there.

—∿∿—

Travelers at the Spring

Fern-edged waters in a woodland spring,
Where forest birds come to drink and sing.
Through arch of trees, the sun bright-laced
Throws mist to rainbows where waters dance
And tumble out with tinkling song,

To a gentler music as they flow along,
Polishing pebbles smooth as glass,
Making ripples as they rise and pass.
Waters distilled from roots of flowers,
Gathering dew and sky-drenched showers
From earth dark-severe into silver pools,
Thirst-quenching, sweet and crystal cool.

Come weary traveler, pause here awhile,
Rest from your journey of many a mile;
Leave off your hurry, toss out your care,
Breathe in the fragrance of leaf-fresh air.

Bend down beside the rock-ribbed brink,
Fill your cup to the brim and deeply drink.

—…—

Old House

The house is old. Two hundred years
Of life has echoed in these halls.
Generations have lived and died
Within the shelter of its walls.

Upon the wide and winding stairs
Fair women have walked down in grace.
The gilt-framed mirror in the hall
Has reflected face on face.

Within the sofa's carved, curved arms,
Many have sat to chat and rest.

And the wide fireplace where flames dance,
Has often warmed both host and guest,
In the doorways darkened arch,
It would seem a figure stood—

When firelight shadows leap & turn
From the crackling, gleaming wood.
There are sounds in this old house—

Footsteps pass on hall & stairs,
And voices in speech & song,
Fainter than faint from everywhere.

—⁓⁓—

My Green Hills

I long to go to the hills again,
To far-off hills & lone,
And walk along the trailways
That I had so well known.

All I would ask is the pathway
That spirals up to the crest
Well, here & there a fallen log
Where I might pause to rest.

I know that along the upward course,
The same beauty would be found,
Far-off glimpses through the trees,
Bright branches forking from the ground,

The air yet sweet with fragrance
Of leaf and fern and pine,
With rocks still holding fast,
And the tangled, clambering vine.

My green hills are waiting,
The same never recedes below,
I long to know these hills again,
I must follow the need to go.

Over the water & under the sky
The river floats green & the boats ride by.
The river is grey & the river is wide
And blue green the hills on either side.

Blue green the hills, nestling fair
A village belonging eternally there
As if there could be no other place
The town could sit with so much grace.

And ever beyond a rippling sheer
And the river, sailing through,
A grey-green path where boats can ride
With the blue hills stretching on either side.

—⟶∾∽⟵—

Maybe Forever?

Each time we part we think it is forever,
We lose each other as
swimmers in a stream
As waves may rise & toss,

Yet now a gleam,
Then suddenly we are
once more together
And then again to part,
Yet stays the dream.

Shall we in time to
Come, our striving over,
Find ourselves upon
some lovely distant shore.

Where silver sands have
heaped their shining store
And both look up in new surprise
to find ourselves together!

With parting waters
not
to slip between us
anymore?

———∽∽∽———

Golden Moon Melon

The moon is a golden melon,
Placed on a cloth of blue;
And if we could only cut it,
We'd have a feast for two.

But the month strolls by and nibbles,
Upon it bite by bite,
And feasts on golden moon melon,
Every single night.

Until upon the cloth of sky,
All that you can find;
Of the tempting melon,
Is a slender, golden rind.

—✶—

The End Is Sleep

The darkness is down and lights in the town,
Make each towered window a star;
By bus and by train, in hurry to gain
Home quickly, crowds scurry afar.

So crowded by day, from skyscrapers away,
The workers in hurry depart;
Brief freedom they know and they hasten to go
To things that are close to their heart.

The day's work is done and now for their fun,
Each one as they have a mind;
Some seek dance and song, and others may long
For all quiet and rest they can find.

Let each as he will his free hours fill,
His dual destiny keep;
But early or late, what else be his fate,
He must yield to the claimant, Sleep.

Tall dark buildings tower high,
And make their mark against the sky,
Crowding out the stately space,
Giving night a man-made face;

While the city's clustered light
Makes fainter the far dome of night.
Yet a patch of sky is there,
Strewn with stars and velvet fair.

Treasures

When you see a lovely poem,
In magazine or daily press;

A picture stark; words apt and clever,
Thoughts, a phrase that you would stress;

Let them not be lost forever,
But clip and paste within a book,

Thoughts they hold are things to treasure,
Holding beauty, life and pleasure,

Put them in some treasure nook.

—*w*—

Journeys Old and New

Old thoroughfares knew the beat
Of horses hoofs on cobbled street;
Highways were rutted and dusty brown,
And wagon wheels marked ways to town.

Carriage, buggy, phaeton or cart,
To arrive in time took an early start;
Echo of old steam whistles blow.
If the journey was far to go,
It was travel long to travel far,
Steamer, stagecoach or railroad car.

A trip that once took weeks to make,
Means but hours for us to take;
Miles between is time between,
Lights turn red, and lights flash green.

Taxi, motor car, bus or truck,
A quick turn and pedestrians duck;
On macadam roads the motors roll
Outward bound, and pay a toll.

—◠◡◠—

Love

Love can be so many things,
Love can be a light,
Love can be a star,
Shining through the night;

Love can be so many things,
Love can be like shining wings.

Love can be so many things,
Love can be a flame,
Love can be a melody
Echoing one name;

Love can be so many things,
Love can be a bird that sings.

Love can be so many things,
Like flowers, memory,
Cherished hours,
Love can be so many things,

As magic flings.

Legend

Winter's pale birches bare, so bare they seem
The silver ghosts of light in which the eyes,
Look and are lost, yet bear a melting frost
Of frailest green upon their brittle trees.

From tree to tree the night-birds call and weave
With cries quick as their flight over factories
Of slow, sudden rising smoke that skips pale looms
Winged shuttles that design their random play.

Well-deep the stillness where the brooks briefly camp
Like clinking stones so heard, a monotone
Of light. All distance lies half-dreamed, dwell
Far sunlight hoists a castle on a flag.

Night early brought her life a verge of green
Between the light-ashen forest & the fields.
And here from golden-furrowed valleys shown
Beside his dreaming stood the lost huntsman.

His hair is golden; his face is pale;
Dark eyes smile at the country loneliness.
The look as if he never will again
Could strike stone, tree & flower, earth to stay.

He feels the sun's brief force on his hands,
Its deep serenity that guides his living.
Leads him from labyrinths of dread on this
Calm pilgrimage towards a lyric song.

He passes, lets his horse go free; for deep
In the veined forest the eldritch song
Leans keen as flint treasure hints & slivers
Wider & sweet. O, listen to the end.

———⟨∿∿⟩———

Instruction to Myself

Be as the moon, that pale far goddess of the night;
Be as the moon, that ever gathers light
From that undwindling source of light, the sun,
But lets the turbulent clouds pass over one by one,

And, however all enveloping they might seem,
With darkness to shut out every moon-bright gleam,
Still knows that clouds can never linger long,
No matter how they crowd and throng;

And then the moon, as scattering clouds drift by,
Will, in re-emerging, ride as high;
Untouched, unmarred, in full serenity glow,
And undelayed on destined pathway go.

Any unknown hidden path
Ever beckons me;
And I should like to take a ship
On some uncharted sea.

Whenever the wind is calling,
I would leave the friendly light,
And people and music and dancing,
And go into the night.

Wherever the moonlight is falling down,
I know this inner need;
To follow, ever follow,
Wherever it may lead.

—⁓⁓⁓—

Fingers of the Wind

The fingers of the wind
Make music all day long;
Gently touching leaves and grass,
Or grasping branches strong;

Turning sounds in passing by,
To chorale or tender song;
The vines that happen in their path,
Must their own music yield;

They shake the bells on flowers,
In garden, wood or field,
And like a mighty orchestra,
The changing power they wield

With variation loud or soft,
In tempo fast or slow,
To an ever moving baton,
With percussion, reed or bow,

The breath and fingers of the wind,
Make music where they go.

—◈—

"The pears are golden in the noon,
And heavy on the boughs."

Heavy on the boughs,
Hang the gold-rich pears,
An amber-flecked necklace
That early autumn wears.

Pendulous they swing,
Warmed by the sun at noon,
Pick and eat one bite by bite,
Or scoop with golden spoon.

Ripened to perfection,
A gourmet's taste to suit,
Reach for all that you can hold,
And feast on nectared fruit.

River Ride

Over the river and under the sky,
The river floats green and boats ride by;

The river is green and the river is wide,
And blue-green the hills on either side;

Green-blue the hills and nestling fair,
A village belonging exactly there,

As if there could be no other place,
The town could sit with so much grace;

And ever beyond the rippling blue,
Are hills with the river cutting through;

A grey-green path where the boats can ride,
With the blue hills stretching on either side.

The Scroll

I stood entranced as in a dream,
Within the luminescent gleam;
Facing the others an angel stood,
Who held both scroll and holy rood;

Four wings he had, all realms to fly,
Hair flaming gold, eyes like the sky;
Robes and wings iridescent bright,
And a halo formed of rainbow light;

Cherubim to seraphim were there,
Angels of all realms, divinely fair;
The heavenly congress paused intent,
On their leader—all eyes were bent,

While on the scroll he held unbound,
Letters and symbols of light were found;
He spoke to them in sacred word,
And all of the assembly heard;

His voice was music but so strange,
I could not follow its least range;
The meanings he could not impart
To me, but etched upon my heart,

Or burned in symbols on my soul,
Are all the secrets of the scroll.

—◦◦◦—

Nocturne

The little winds are walking in the gardens of the night,
Here and there a white-winged moth makes its nocturnal flight;
The fountain catches silver from the silver towered moon,
And dancing in the darkness makes a tinkling, tumbling tune.

All the fragrant, sleeping blossoms are telling where they go,
Spilling out their fragrance as soft winds stir and go;
While the night blooming flowers with petals white and frail;
Mark their presence in the garden, banked and drifted silver pale;

Leafy shadows go dancing on the moonlit garden wall;
A wakened bird makes a small and fluttered call;
Moonlight and shadow intermingling, while the soft winds know
Fragrance of all the flowers, and music as they go.

—⁓—

White

White holds a world of wonder—
Falling snow, that covers earth
With its white hush;
Whipped white clouds, that change
And shape as winds may go;

White fringes on the water,
As it churns, or waves may leap and fall.
Creamy pearls with lovely luster,
And white roses with their
Petaled fragrance;

Daises to whiten a field at dusk,
And Queen Anne's Lace beside a road.
A drift of white moonflower,
Pale against a garden wall,
With a white moon to blossom
In a dusky sky;

White words like peace and gentleness,
And ivory white piano keys
That hold a wealth of music.
Alabaster and ivory carved
By loving fingers, and marble
Sculpted to the pale beauty of a dream.

—⁓—

The Best We Can

What use to frown when things go wrong,
Since frowns don't set them right;
Be brave of heart and sing a song
To make the burden light.
That this is true I quite believe:

He is the wisest man
Who sings when care and trouble come
And does the best he can.

Brood over trouble and you will find
The burden heavier grows,
Those who let worry have its way
Have always found it so.
He gathers flowers beside the way
Who says to fellowman:
"Let's make the most of pleasant things
And do the best we can."

In thinking of another's need
We oft forget our own,
By helping others with their load
Two hearts have cheerful grown.
So try to scatter by the way
Some good for fellowman,
And with a smile of courage say:
"I'll do the best I can.

———∽∾∽———

Autumn Night

Beyond the fringe of pines,
The low winds moan;
But here in my garden
Where I stand alone,

The night seems strangely hushed,
As the winds sound afar.
While above the towering hill,
Gleams a blue-white star;

Like a brightly fringed lamp,
As the clouds drift by,
The moon is silver shaded,
Climbing up the sky;

The stars seem scattered wide,
The night winds blow;
There is mist in the air;
And the trees bend low;

But here in my garden
Where I stand alone,
The night is hushed and still,
There are only petals blown

From the last of the roses
That have lingered on,
Though the leaves from the trees
Have drifted and gone;

Only the tall chrysanthemums
Are shaking their heads,
As the dry grass is rustling
Round the flower beds;

Only a wakeful starling
Is chirping low,
As the winds of autumn
Drift and blow;

The garden seems to sleep,
And is strangely still;
Though trees are bending in the wind,
And clouds sweep by.

———

What Lies Under?

The sea is wild and the sea is deep,
With treasures to hold and secrets to keep.
How many tons of sunken gold?
How many ships that were fair and bold,

That never found their way to shore,
But are fathoms below on the ocean floor?
How many lives lost through the years,
How much grief and how many tears?

For storm winds blow and waves heave high,
Drowning the echo of each cry.
How many cities and how much land,
Downed by the sea as it swallows sand?

Only the waves and the winds can tell,
Every secret guarding well.
Only the deep sea fishes know
Of the treasures that lie below,

Held in the grip of coral caves,
Far beneath the sound of the waves,
Lit by strange phosphorescent glow,
That trail sea creatures as they go.

For the sea is wild and the sea is deep,
With treasures to hold and secrets to keep.

—⁓—

Passage

Death is an ending and a beginning,
A letting go, and new worlds winning;

Death is a ship with sunset sails,
Outward blown past earthly gales;

Death is a passport for one alone,
That leads to harbours now unknown;

Death is the passage that leads to new birth,
Ascending from the dark womb of earth;

Before is the bulb, after the flower,
To bloom in glory a heavenly hour;

Death leads the soul to find its wings,
And learn to drink from immortal springs,

Where life can know the speed of light,
Untrammeled, free, and rainbow bright.

—⁓⁓—

No Fragility

There is no fragility to lovely things
Though in flight as swift as passing wings;
From color of a cloud, or flower's breath,
To face of one much loved though lost in death;

From sound of music echoing in the heart,
To all the woven threads that make a part
Of every life; a thought of tenderness
To richest wonder of love's deep caress;

All cherished things that slip into the past,
Potent with greater purpose may yet last,
If in one heart their beauty is inscribed,
Or if there is one soul who has imbibed

A treasured memory to hold and keep;
One human being to respond, whose pulses leap
To color, motion, meaning, shape or sound,
All that has seeming vanished may be found

In transmutation to the finer gold,
That living thought may ever keep and hold,
Even as symboled Grecian torch is handed on,
Bearer to bearer to light the flames of dawn;

Not only atom may chain reaction know,
But all that touches life will constant flow
As each life touches others, shaping ways
By which men walk the avenue of days.

Response to Music

Music is like the rising sea,
With sweeping tides of melody,
Engulfing us in harmony.

Music is like a wind to blow,
Softly at first, then rising slow
Till its wide sweep is all we know.

Music is like a growing light
To break the silence, as the night
Is broken by the dawn, rose-bright.

Slowly at first, till rising sound
Seems to lift us from the ground,
While soul and senses start to pound.

Till we are caught within its spell
As chord and cadence strike and swell,
And in a world all music dwell.

Then silence, now, is not the same,
Nor do our senses seem quite tame,
While darkness glows with hidden flame.

"WITHIN REACH
WHO CAN NET THE RUNNING TIDE,
HOLD WINDS AS THEY GO FREE?
OR LASSO CLOUDS DOWN FROM THE SKY
AND CART WAVES FROM THE SEA?"

But each may gather bright sea shells,
find raindrops in a drop of dew,
Or smell the fragrance of all flowers
As wings blow them to you.

We can hear the white tipped waves,
Pounding on a sandy beach,
While eyes can keep the shifting sands,
And all the sky in reach.

Of these we can keep pictures,
And weave notes into song,
Or make with words a poem,
And wind and waves keep long.

(Dedicated to Prof. Victor DeLisa, Patron-Composer to the Poets)

Joy of Living

I would not wish for Heaven now,
With all the blossoms on the bough;
While earth is filled with lilt of song,
And many roads to choose among.

There is so much of beauty near,
The light of Heaven shines even here.
If blind to treasures earth might hold,
How can we vision Heaven's gold?

If hearts cannot heap high with love,
Shall they hold more in realms above?
If hands do not work now with will,
Can Heaven give them greater skill?

May loved ones' faces be more dear
In Heaven than they can be here,
Or God Himself be closer by?
For know that He is ever nigh,

And this His world as much as any,
However far worlds are and many.
Here is found the joy of living,
Of seeing, knowing, loving, giving.

You do not go to Heaven, you grow—
A self to be and do and know.
Your immortality is now,
With all the blossoms on the bough.

Sea Call

The night is still, the stars are far,
And far is the whispering sea,
The winds are still, the night birds call,
And I hear the call of the sea.

Silent the night and distant the sea,
But I hear the surging of far off waves,
And the see the entrance of deep sea caves,
With the ocean pouring in........

Always I hear the ocean song,
And before me sea lanes beckon and throng,
Whenever I walk on moonlit paths,
When the stars are far and the sea is far,
And the winds and the night are still.

———◦◦◦———

Rising

Slowly at first, till rising sound
Seems to lift us from the ground,
While soul and senses start to pound.

Till we are caught within its spell,
As chord and cadence strike and swell.
And in a world all music dwell.

Then slower, fainter, come the beats,
While the wealth of sound retreats,
Till memory's ear alone repeats.

Yet silence now is not the same,
Nor do our senses seem quite tame,
While darkness glows with hidden flame.

Long shall these threads of melody,
And all the throb of harmony,
Resound within the memory.

Childhood By The River

Often we walked beside the singing river,
The river that was little more than stream;
But we called it river and strolled beside it,
And paused sometimes to watch a silver gleam

As playful trout leaped to the surface;
Or else we stood waiting turn to throw
Smooth pebbles, singly or a winging handful,
Eager to see the spreading ripples go;

There were cool rocks to sit upon and watch
A family of ducks go swimming by,
While now and then, darting among the cat-tails,
Whirred blue metallic wings of dragonfly.

A Changing Song

All things must pass, a flower or a star,
That which was far comes near, and near...the far;
All that we know has on it touch of doom,
Each mortal thing must go, thus making room
So that which is to come may be,
For life and love- are both one flowing melody;
Not any of it held for over-long,
For everything is but a changing song.
Farewell winter, welcome spring,
When all the birds come back and sing;
Farewell silence, welcome song,
May sorrow be brief and joy be long.

Magic Apples

My pockets are empty, but the gold I want
Is the gold at the rainbow's end;
Though I gather the silver I find on the way,
Or coppers earned in a toilsome day,
They can never my fortunes really mend,
For I want the gold at the rainbow's end.

I have not eaten for many a day,
There are feast tables filled
And those who say, "Stay!"......
But greater the hunger I must know then,
For that magical fruit beyond the seas,
The apples of gold from the Hesperides.

Oh the small loves come and the small loves go,
To melt as flakes of fallen snow,
And all they can do is reveal the gleam
That shines from a once forgotten dream,
A love all-embracing, and far
As the rainbow's gold or a long-lost star,
And the magic apples beyond the seas,
The golden fruit of the Hesperides.

～∾～

Ever Free

I have one foot that's a wandering foot,
To follow the roads away,
For I would be going over the hills,
Ever at break of day.

And I have one foot that's a stay at home foot,
And never seeks to roam;
That when I'm gone as I must be gone,
Is ever urging me home.

I have one hand that would turn the wheel,
Ever to ways unknown,
That would lead me to unchartered seas,
Swept by the fates, wind-blown.

And I have one hand that's a home keeping hand,
To garden and cook and sew;
A hand that would ever busy itself
With seeking to build, not go.

I have but one heart, and part of my heart
Is held by the hills and the sea;
Although I ache to be claimed by love,
My heart must be ever free.

Drink Deep the Rose

Take treasure from the flowing moment,
Before it changing goes
Drink deep the beauty of the Rose,
The dawns, the days, the songs.
Know fragrance of each summer day,-
Though lost on winds of Time it blows,
Yet in your soul may all the beauty stay.

—⟨⟩—

The Bird of Dawn

Rising from its nest of night,
Like some great wild bird seeking flight;
The dawn lifts up rose-tinted crest,
And shakes bright feathers from its breast;
Looks on the world with a golden eye,
And lifts its wings into the sky.

—⟨⟩—

The Nicest Place

The nicest place is always where you are;
Beneath high noon or underneath a star;

Walking by day or night on city streets,
Or wandering where land and river meets;

Sailing upon a wide lake's blue expanse,
Or driving out to country inn to dance;

Sitting on any bench in any park;
Or holding hands just somewhere in the dark;

In any room I find myself with you;
Or else together at a table made for two;

Whether it keeps me here or takes me far;
The nicest place is always where you are.

—◊—

Dream Ships

Everyone has their dream ship,
Laden with all they love best;
It may be with hopes for the future,
Or cargoes where memories rest;
Every heart has its treasure;
Dream ships upon their wide quest.

To all there's a land of magic,
Where opened are many doors,
And broad seas where there are floating,
Dream boats filled with golden stores,
Cargoes of secret hopes and dreaming,
Sailing to far off shores.

Moon-grey waters caress the silver sands,
Dream ships come sailing from magic lands;
Treasure ships laden with the gist of years,
Beauty and laughter, and love and tears;
While silver clouds drift above the silver foam:
Dream ships are bringing their treasure home.

Goal

I am not one for little loves,
Or conquests here and there;
For there is one to whom I belong,
To whom I gave myself when time began,
Mine out of all the world,
Heaven and earth and life and love to me,
To whom I yield myself as dew to sunlight,
Whose soul with mine, shall mount the stars,
Until our spirits mingle and are one.

⌇⌇

Sunset Aisle

Green arches, interlacing, spread
Above dim aisles that lead
To western altars where the tired Sun,
Sinking upon the bosom of the Earth,

Melts into seas of rose mists.
The flute call of a thrush is heard
Above the bassoon of a lone frog.
The hushed choir of a thousand voices

Throbs in the early twilight.
The cloud-shaded lamps fade out,
Gold and rose pale to mauve,
And Earth is wrapped in veils of dusk.

—⁓⁓—

Glad Blue

Earth seems made of blue today,
Blue are the hills and blue the bay;
Arching above is wide blue sky,
And blue the far sea reaches,
Blue curls the water around the rocks
That stand blue-grey on sandy beaches;

To eat our picnic lunch upon,
I've even brought blue dishes,
While swimming near to nibble crumbs,
Silver blue are little fishes;
Green blue the spruce that edge the shore,

More blue in stretching far;
This flower that I found and plucked,
Is like a small blue star;
While bluer than any blue your eyes;
My world glad blue from sea to skies.

Young Orangutang

She does not know that she is wild,
She thinks she is a human child;
She always has good things to eat,
And now and then a special treat:
She tries her tricks, climbs ceiling high,
The cynosure of every eye.
Despite orangutanish ways,
Each thing she learns to do wins praise.

Yet present home will not remain,
Once body has outgrown her brain;
There will be nothing else to do,
But send her to live in a zoo.

And will she beat her bars in rage,
To find herself held in a cage?
Then later, will it compensate,
When she shares it with a mate;
In man's house she now takes ease,

While her young apish antics please,
Though she could climb up any steeple,
She no doubt thinks she is "people".
All her instincts now are mild,
She does not know that she is wild.

—◈—

A Tale of Old (Prologue)

Listen, while I tell a tale of old;
A story of love, war, and gold,
Of a ship that sailed from London town,
And a girl in a rose brocaded gown,
Of a Spanish ship and a pirate ship,
Of treasure, of cutlass, of the lash of a whip,
Of a gentleman and a pirate crew,
And what an English girl could do.

1.

In the sixteenth century there lived a maiden fair,
Rosamunde Trent of the golden brown hair,
She was loved by the son of an English lord,
Young Sir John of Havercroft with his shining new sword;
This pair of lovers met to say goodbye;
She smiled although she wanted to cry;
They talked of the new world, they talked of the old,
He wanted to gain a fortune in gold;
He asked her some day to be his bride,
In the morning he sailed on the bright blue tide.

2.

His ship was called the Elizabeth Jane,
The vessel sailed the Spanish Main;
The topsails filled, the sails blew out,
The men aboard gave a merry shout,
As they sailed at break of day,
And out of the harbor they slipped away.
The year was fifteen hundred and eighty four,
England and Spain were then at war,

And all went well for a month and a day
Until the lookout came to say,
"There's a Spanish ship on the horizon,
Prepare to fight or try to outrun."
Each filled his pistol and sharpened his sword,
And among them this son of an English lord.

3.
The ship glared fiery in the light of dawn,
Each man his sword and musket drawn,
As on the waves she closer came,
They could make out the letters of her name;
The plumed Dons were waiting, too;
As ever closer on she drew;
Then there was a clash with shout,
That soon became a bloody rout,
They fought, the hours went slowly by,
Many there were who fell to die,
Until at last their captain went,
And soon the battle's force was spent,
While there nigh on the close of day,
In the Spaniard's hold the prisoners lay.

———✦———

Call to Outdoors

Leave your books and come outside,
September skies are very blue, the world is wide,
And there is air that has the tang of wine;
The outdoors waits; still green the sod,
Many paths are ready for your feet to trod,
And for your hands to gather, grapes on the vine.

To look far upon, there stands a purple hill,
To match the purple thistle by the mill,
Where tumbles down a sparkling waterfall;
The fields of ripening grain are golden seas,
And more of sunlight glances through the thinning trees,
That bear upon their shoulders touch of early fall.

Let all of indoors wait. Come then and know
The place where scarlet flag and purple aster grow;
Let sweet September winds blow cobwebs off your brain;
The world's wide loveliness to know and feel is yours;
The outdoors calls. Let it not call in vain,
But know the glad, wild ways of youth again.

Winter Fire

Pile on the logs and light the fire,
And bring the chairs to circle around;
As the tiny flames catch hold,
There comes a crackling sound;

A bit of wood smoke in the air,
While small flames reach and grow,
Until with color, light and warmth
The fire logs brightly glow.

I thought fall's brilliant colors gone,
But here (from wood they leap),
For warmth of sun and autumn flame,
The quiet logs hold and keep.

Spring Wonder

I feel spring wonder stir in me
When the signs of spring appear;
Buds unfolding on a tree,
Changes in the atmosphere.

When the signs of spring appear,
As sun warmed earth and new green make
Changes in the atmosphere,
Now sleeping roots have come awake.

As sun warmed earth and new green make
A place for blossoms to appear,
Now sleeping roots have come awake
With leaf and flower fragrance near.

A place for blossoms to appear
When forsythia spears are gold,
With leaf and flower fragrance near,
Crocus and hyacinth unfold.

When forsythia spears are gold,
With tulips bright upon the stalk,
Crocus and hyacinth unfold,
Birds come with song and mating talk.

With tulips bright upon the stalk,
The leaves of trees seem pale green lace,
Birds come with song and mating talk,
Make of boughs a nesting place.

The leaves of trees seem pale green lace;
Buds unfolding on a tree
Make of boughs a nesting place;
I feel spring wonder stir in me.

Flow

Rivers are like life, they flow
And on their channeled courses go,
Reflecting, where waters are serene,
Facets of the passing scene;

Sunlight touches them with gold,
Strange things within their depths to hold,
Up and down the river boats ride,
Bridges cross from side to side.

Yet source to sea the rivers know,
One direction in their flow,
Finding as they reach the sea,
Fulfillment of their destiny.

—✺—

Mountain Sunset

At last we reached the mountain's peak,
And gladly took our rest,
For we had climbed for hours,
Up the mountain's rocky breast.

Groping, reaching, climbing,
Securing every hold;
It was delight now to relax,
And watch the skies unfold.

Such glorious sight we saw beyond,
A rich reward we knew,
With peaks and ranges reaching out,
Full far as we could view.

There snow-capped peaks caught rainbow light,
Beneath the sunset fires,
Into rose flaming clouds,
Reached rose flushed mountain spires.

Till touching cloud and mountain,
The purpling twilight came,
And silently and swiftly,
Quenched all there was of flame.

—*&*—

Pulse of Wonder

Every season has its part,
As the endless rhythms flow
In the beat of Nature's heart.

Roots awake with spring and start
The rising sap that leaf may grow;
Every season has its part.

Summer is a flower mart,
Blossom fragrant breezes blow
In the beat of Nature's heart.

Autumn comes, fulfills the chart,
With reaped harvest it can show;
Every season has its part.

Piercing winds of winter dart,
Yet earth knows coverlet of snow,
In the beat of Nature's heart.

Each cycle a recurring start,
Seeds must fall to newly sow;
Every season has its part,
In the beat of Nature's heart.

Seed Cycle (Haiku)

The seed falls to earth
Holding the plant in its heart;
New flower, fruit, seed.

—⁓—

Cycle of the Seed

Seeds in the earth break for their nourishing,
Sending out roots to absorb and hold;
Tendrils stem upward, find light for flourishing,
Sending out leafage and bud to unfold.

Knowing sunlight and the rain's showering,
Earth, light, air, water to meet each need;
Finding fulfillment in fragrance and flowering,
And storing all wonder within the new seed.

—⁓—

Remembered Roadway

The roadway circled around the hill
Like a wedding ring;
From the town and back to town,
It was a road for following.

On one side woods and hillside slope,
The other, green fields looking down,
Past farms and grazing lands,
To river-ribboned valley and the town.

In woods close by wildflowers grew,
Arbutus, violet, columbine;
With green of moss and fretted fern,
And tangled honeysuckle vine.

Here was sight and sound of birds,
What better place for nesting?
If wearied walking, you could find
A fallen log for resting.

Before you knew it you would come,
To where the roadway's both ends meet.
The place where they join
To find the downward street.

Yet always for remembering,
The roadway like a wedding ring.
Before we knew it we had come
To where the circle was complete
And the roadway both ends joined
To find the downward street.

Lights At Night

Night with its darkness settles down,
Lights blossom out all over town;
The street lamps glow with yellow light,
To show you city streets by night;

And lighted windows star the dark,
Here outline a building; mark
The curving bridge; lights move slow
As up and down the river boats may go;

Here and there the headlight
Of a moving car makes bright
A stretch of road; within the square
Lights throw a circle on the grass, and dare

To trim the shadows; the small pool
Has netted stars, the night is full
Of scattered lights, half-round the world;
With overhead the star-strewn sky unfurled.

Wealth

These things are wealth,
Eyes to see beauty,
Ears to hear the music of the world,
A mind to understand,
And love.

Welcome to the Someday House

When you come to "Someday House"
I shall wait to welcome you;
There will be many happy things
That we shall find to do.
I'll watch you coming up the path
And up to my front door;
I'll let you sound the knocker,
Then wait a minute more....

I'll take your coat and hang it up,
And in the deepest cushioned chair;
You'll settle down to rest awhile,
While I shall bring blue willow ware
To place upon a table near,
Sandwiches, and your favorite cake,
A bowl of fruit, which will you take?
This bunch of grapes, a pear of gold,

Or might a polished apple hold
The most appeal....
Rich and fragrant, here's a pot
Of finest coffee, steaming hot—
Which I shall pour in these two cups...
After you have rested quite,
And we have talked a space,
I'll take you over and around
And all about the place,
When you have come to "Someday House"
And I have welcomed you.

Hallowe'en

Tonight the witches ride,
And ghosts and goblins wander;
Light up the Jack-o-Lantern,
And hope to keep them yonder.

Tonight the witches ride,
And you may learn your fate;
Walk backward down the cellar stairs,
Mirror may show your future mate.

Tonight the witches ride,
On many an eerie task;
Fool them by wearing costume,
And don't forget your mask.

Tonight the witches ride,
And ghouls may walk the night;
Come quickly to the ball,
And dance by lantern light.

Conch Shell Song

The conch shell shows the curve of wave,
And holds in its heart strange memories;
It echoes all the sea has known,
Its whispering melodies.
Hold to your ear and listen well,
While enchanted sails outbound,
Transport you to far sea wonder,
Sea visions... and sea sound...

Hear the wild sea-horses ride,
Hoof beats pounding with the tide,
And their neighing as they plunge,
Breakers turning, bending under,
Against far shores with their thunder;
Ancient galleons still sail,
And the Triton's trumpets wail,
Far-blown to echo over vast

Sea reaches and the mast
Of sunken ship may rise once more,
With all their crew, and cargo's store;
Like dolphins let your fancy leap,
Explore the depths within the deep,
And wander in the sea-green caves,
Fathoms deep beneath the waves;
Rise to the sands of some far isle,

And dream with sea shell songs the while.
Sing to us, conch shell, your music,
That echoes the sea's deep thunder,
And all that you hold within your heart,
Of the ocean's unending wonder;
Deep within the curve of your shell,
Weave for us this age-old spell.

Mountain Symphony

We climbed the hill, nor looked to right nor left,
Until I stopped to see a flower growing in the cleft
Between two barren rocks; I paused —
It must have been a wind-blown seed that caused

This beauty to bloom here; sprouting somehow
The roots reached down and into crevice grew,
And sun and rain and wind the leafing knew,
Until its being in fulfillment now

Had reached the perfect hour,
When bud had opened into full-blown flower;
I knew it not by name but it was fair,
Frail and frosty white as it made sweet the air;

I looked awhile, just once my arm moved out
With reaching fingers; I was about
To pick the blossom; but drew my hand away,
To be glad ever after that I let this beauty stay,

Where venturesome small seed had found itself a space,
And growing to flower here had lent the rocks its grace.

—◦◦◦—

Trails of Fantasy

When I walk on city streets,
I may wander wide and far;
Walk barefoot in meadowlands,
Or dance from star to star.

I may step on distant shore,
Treading on silver-sanded dune,
Or go, thought-swift, to wander on
The mountains of the moon.

I might visit China,
And ride the hills of Spain,
Or travel back into the past
To childhood roads again;

I may return to Babylon,
Or ancient Egypt's Nile,
For all the past and future,
Dreams within each mile;

You may see me walking past,
But you will never know,*
On what far trails of fantasy,
I may, singing, go....

*unless I write a poem about it! DN

―⟆⟆⟆―

April Music

April winds are crooning songs,
My heart is singing, too;
April sings to all the world,
My songs are to you.

April songs are of the earth,
Enchantment of the spring,
Blue skies and fragrant blossoms,
Birds to nest and sing.

All my songs are love songs,
Romance makes the theme,
Star spun enchanted magic,
Spilling from a dream.

April's making music,
My heart is singing, too;
All my songs are love songs,
Melodies for you.

Story of a Street

It started as a foot path through fields of clover,
From meadowland to woods, down to the brook and over;
Curved past a flat topped rock where man and beast rested,
And near the tangled vines where wild grouse nested.

A farmhouse was built and there were fields of grain,
The slender path through clover widened to Clover Lane;
The woods became a clearing with a church standing there,
Little houses clustered into a village square.

Tall houses crowded, stores and a school were built,
The town became a city with streets brightly lit;
Landmarks were torn down to make place for the new,
A hotel and apartments, a restaurant or two.

Yet if you walk on Clover Street and keep going over,
Looking closely by the curb, you'll find a bit of clover.

———⟿———

Color Therapy

Yesterday I dressed in blue,
The hours were glad and gay;
Today I wear a gown of red,
To ease the pain of tears I've shed.

—◦◦◦—

Gift of Love

My love is always with you,
A mantle, a shield and a song;
It tenderly enfolds you,
To comfort, protect and make strong.

—◦◦◦—

Love Song

You shed a light on all of life for me,
The stars shine brighter and the earth makes melody;
When I am with you, the silence sings,
The sunlight dances in me, and I soar on wings
Of love, to heights of ecstasy;
I seem to float upon a golden sea
Where love and light and music all are one;

You are the earth, the moon, the stars, the sun;
I love you utterly and I could be no less true
Than stars upon their courses sweeping through
The vastnesses of space.
My heart is like a shrine
Where only you may enter, my love a light to shine
Undimmed, illuminating all I think or do.
This is my love for you.

—◈—

The Haunted Garden

The little winds that softly go,
In this old garden surely know
Of things that happened long ago.

It seems that by this carved sun dial,
The winds might pause to tarry awhile,
Remembering a young girl's smile.

She who once stood near lupines tall,
Has portrait hanging on the wall,
In yonder dark ancestral hall.

But one with this sweet and laughing face,
And manner that is full of grace,
Must much prefer this garden place.

Though now no summer flower grows,
Yet fragrance of mignonette and rose
Stirs as the wind so gently goes.

The little winds so softly sigh,
You hear, almost, faint voices draw nigh,
And little, tripping steps go by.

———

Old Trees

There is something about old trees,
That quiets the restless soul,
And clarifies the vision
To seek an ancient goal.

There is something like a temple here,
In tall and quiet peace;
While from the world's turbulence,
There is gained release.

These trees that knew the centuries,
For pain and fear hold balm,
Beneath their templed arches,
Is found an inner calm.

From these sturdy boughs, it seems
There comes an inner flow,
And losing weariness and strife,
We, too, in stature grow.

There is something about old trees,
Like pillars of a church they stand,
Bring man close to things divine,
Building a temple on the land.

—⁓⁓—

Cloud Changes

Within the east unfolds the dawn,
And morning robes the clouds put on,
Gladly discard garments of night,
To clad themselves in colors bright;
Palest pink to flame they wear,
With glittering bandeaus in their hair,
But all too soon their colors fade,
In work-a-day white they must parade
Across the clearing blue of sky,

While the sun glares with his golden eye;
But if the sun should hide away,
They mostly wear raincoats of grey,
Or else turn themselves to rain,
Until the sun comes out again;
Then when the sun dips in the west,
They hurry on their evening best,
Amethyst satin, velvet rose,

Some have silver slippers on their toes,
And now and then a happy cloud may wear,
An early star to hold in place her hair;
Their long day over, they are free to go,
So off they dance into the afterglow.

Autumn Cinquain

Autumn winds
Dance with the leaves
And carry them off
In bright golden rain
On October earth.

Autumn winds
Shake down the gold
From the thinning trees
To spread a carpet
Across October.

Autumn winds
Blow drying leaves
Into scattered heaps
To make a cover
For sleeping flowers.

Autumn winds Stir the grasses
And shake flower stalks,
Tossing out the seeds
For future growth.

Autumn winds turn to music
Sound from drying grass,
Tree branch and stirring leaves
Lulling to winter sleep.

These Are The Things

With you in mind, I'll plan my life;
And all the things that we might do;
With you in mind, I'll set my goals
For all that I might share with you.

With you in mind, I'll shape myself,
And all that I may have or be;
These are the things that I shall seek,
And strive and care for tenderly.

That if you wish to enter in,
And our lives together share;
You'll find a hearth fire to be lit,
A table with your favorite fare.

You'll find full loveliness at hand,
And of life's gifts, all of the best;
That here you may find all you seek,
And all to make you happiest.

—⟨∞⟩—

Love Song

You shed a light on all of life for me,
The stars shine brighter and the earth makes melody;
When I am with you the silence sings,
The sunlight dances in me, and I soar on wings
Of love, to heights of ecstasy;
I seem to float upon a golden sea
Where love and light and music all are one;

You are the earth, the moon, the stars, the sun;
I love you utterly, and I could be no less true
Than stars upon their courses sweeping through
The vastness of space. My heart is like a shrine
Where only you may enter, my love a light to shine
Undimmed, illuminating all I think or do.
This is my love for you.

City

From leaning parapet
We view the curving road,
Busy with cars
Traveling the early night;
Darker than the dusk,
They look like racing insects
Of some strange breed,
Somewhat akin to beetles,
And with bulging eyes,
Full of fire; headlights
Staring intent at the road;
At regular intervals,
They are held back briefly
By the crossing lights;
Then released,
To surge in waves,
And plunge along, full of hurry,
Intent on separate goals.

———

Looking High

Tall, dark buildings tower high,
And mark their angles on the sky,

Crowding out much starry space,
Giving night a man-made face,

While the city's clustered light,
Makes fainter the far dome of night.

Yet a patch of sky is there,
Stitched with stars and velvet fair,

Lights to send their ancient gleam,
That all who will look high may dream.

Snow Petals

So soft they fell, so frail and fair,
These snowflakes on the April air,
No less than blossom petals they seemed,
As softly in the sun they gleamed.

Gossamer white they drifted by
As though some tree shook in the sky,
With petaled drift, through the perfume
From budding trees and flowers in bloom.

I looked to see them on the lawn,
The blossom whiteness all was gone,
And there was only new spring green,
With not a trace of snow petals seen.

Easter Gladness

May gladness unfold like the fragrance of flowers,
Bringing joy to your heart this Easter Day;
All good things to come in profusion of showers,
To lead you along a blossom bright way.

May all of the warmth of the friendship you proffer,
Shine bright as the sunshine on all that you do,
To bring you the finest life has to offer,
With Eastertime happiness all year for you.

—ฌฌฌ—

Place

I shall build my someday house,
With windows open wide
To all the gold of sunshine
That can find its way inside.

The large and friendly kitchen
Will have a window with a view
Of hills and fields and woods
And the sky's own blue.

Gleam of copper pots and pans,
And a red tile floor
With morning glory vines
Growing by the kitchen door.

In a bedroom gay and restful,
And lavender sweet,
Stiff starched curtains for windows
Sparkling fresh and neat.

A place for dining
Where candlelight shall play,
The table with an extra plate
For who may come that way.

Books, music, firelight,
Soft rugs upon the floor
And at the entrance way
A wide and welcome door.

May those who step inside
Always come to know
That here they find some gladness
To take with them when they go.

———∾∾∾———

Response to Music

Music is like the rising sea,
Its sweeping tide of melody,
Engulfing us in harmony.

Music is like a wind to blow
Softly at first, then rising slow
Till its wide sweep is all you know.

Music is like a growing light
To break the silence; as the night
Is broken by the dawn, rose-bright.

Slowly at first till every sound,
Seems to lift us from the ground
And slow and senses start to pound.

Till we are caught within its spell,
As chord and cadence start to swell
And we in music's world may dwell.

Then slower, fainter, near the last,
And all the wealth of sound retreats
And memory, clear alone repeats,

Yet silence is not the same,
Nor are senses yet quite tame
While darkness glows with hidden flame.

Grandmother's Bible

Lamplight softly fell on Grandmother's face,
And on the pages of the Holy Book,
For here, in quiet hours, she would look
For proverb, parable, and word of grace.
The pages of her Bible were well turned,
As over and again she read each page,
For priceless words of prophet and of sage,
These were the sources where she sought and learned.

Her Bible brought into her life a light,
Which because of her illumines mine,
To seek the good and try to do the right,
And tune my soul to hear the song divine;
The things she read and taught became a part
Of all my life, to guide my mind and heart.

—~~~—

Autumn Days

Sing a song of autumn days,
Treasure teems along her ways;
Golden goblets,—apple, pear;
Bite and find the nectar there.

Gorge yourself on grapes, wine-filled,
Heap your arms with treasure spilled
From the harvest everywhere.
Taste the tang of spice-filled air.

Pile the dry leaves, light the fire,
Autumn incense from the spire;
Travel along paths of gold,
Wealth that is not bought nor sold;

Dance upon the golden ways,
To sing a song of autumn days.

———

Temporary Contemporary

Highlights of the passing scene,
Flash and fade on T V screen;
Doings of small and large import,
Told of in the news report;
Reams of newsprint every day,
Repeat the story, sad or gay;
All to fall and fade from view,
And give way to something new,
Yet with trace left in memory,
Or some mark on history.

Time travels on in constant pace,
With much to crowd into brief space;
While endlessly the new turns old,
As wet turns dry, and hot turns cold;
All of it all together,
Like the ever-changing weather;
Equally temporary,
Avant-garde and contemporary;
And what is high style for awhile,
Tomorrow will surely bring a smile.

—⁓—

Telephone

Your voice on the wire can be a magic thing,
It somehow has the power to make my whole world sing,
The dullness swiftly brightens as when sudden sunlight comes,
And in my heart is throbbing like the beating of glad drums.

Your voice on the wire is such a magic thing,
It lifts me to the skies, it has the power to bring
Strength in place of weariness, a smile for a tear;
There's joy where there was sadness, and lovely things seem near.

Your voice on the wire is like a magic thing,
For as you speak, I somehow swiftly wing
From humdrum things to starlight; in sudden ecstasy
I know a swift, sweet rapture that brings you close to me.

With You

It doesn't really matter where we go,
It doesn't really matter what we do;
The only thing that really truly matters,
Are happy hours spent with you.

It doesn't matter if the day is warm or chilly,
It doesn't matter if the skies are grey or blue;
Because the thing that mostly makes the weather,
Is whether or not I can be with you.

It doesn't matter if I'm tired or rested,
Nor greatly, how fair might be the view;
Because the thing that makes all things seem lovely,
Is just - if I can be with you.

Day's End

The sun at last was sinking low,
On farther hills spread ruddy glow,
And warned us that we must depart,
From the hill's peak, full time to start.

On the returning journey's way,
Close as it was to end of day;
We must go now by ebbing light
And hope to reach the town by night.

Yet, first we paused to look across
The valley where night soon would toss
Veiled darkness; it lay deep and wide,
With hills heaped up on every side.

Reluctantly we turned and went
Upon a path so curved and bent
That you could not guess it would go
Into the slopes that lay below.

But there it led; now we must keep
Our eyes on places that were steep.
Go carefully; yet soon we found
A path that led to gentler ground.

Though here and there a rough place loomed,
We went through spots where daisies bloomed,
And here we paused to look about,
And saw the stars were stepping out.

Saw the lights, too, when we looked down,
That here and there showed in the town.
Slower we walked, the night was still,
Behind us stood the darkened hill;

Now that we stood on lower ground,
We could see all the hills surround,
And the valley seemed to rest,
Peaceful and safe as in a nest.

Looking High

Tall, dark buildings tower high,
And angles make against the sky;
But still a patch of sky is there,
Stitched with stars and velvet fair;
Full enough of stars to gleam,
That those who do look high, may dream.

—⁓—

Summer Afternoon

The blue of the bellflower matches the sky,
The white summer phlox is towering high;
Petunias are pink as the flowering dawn,
Green velvet smooth is the grass of the lawn.
Dizzy with pollen the bee makes its way,
With honey collected for all of the day;
The frills of the four o'clock unfold,
While the afternoon sun spills drowsy gold.

—⁓—

Winged Thoughts

Like bright-winged butterflies,
My thoughts so often travel
To bring you wealth of happiness,
And all your cares unravel.

Some are filled with gaiety,
Some carry gentle peace;
There are those to give you strength,
And from weariness release.

Thoughts from all harm to guard you,
Others to bring a song;
That happiness surround you,
Vital, glad and strong.

They bring you all the joy,
That thoughts may ever bring,
For they come straight from my heart,
To make your own heart sing.

Harvest Song

Autumn brings both fruit and seed,
And the gold and scarlet leaves;
Beauty and bread to meet man's need.

Grain for flocks and men to feed,
Wheat tied up in golden sheaves;
Autumn brings both fruit and seed.

Russet rich colors from tree to weed,
Golden bright the pattern weaves;
Beauty and bread to meet man's need.

The season's changes ever speed,
Fruit turns to wine but no one grieves,
Autumn brings both fruit and seed.

Time's nimble footsteps onward lead,
Wind-blown are seeds and gold-brown leaves;
Beauty and bread to meet man's need.

Riches to reward the deed,
Who plants the seed, harvest receives;
Autumn brings both fruit and seed,
Beauty and bread to meet man's need.

Dream Garden

I would have a garden with an old sun-dial,
A place to sit and write, and perhaps dream awhile And watch a
butterfly in lazy, hovering flight,
Like a floating flower as it pauses to alight;

Or a bee buzz by with all he can hold
Of golden grains of flower-pollened gold.
There would be a fountain to strum a tinkling tune, silver stringed
in moonlight, rainbow batons at noon;

And then a quiet place shadow-dim and cool,
Where goldfish swim in a water lily pool;
Rose-colored flowers to greet the morning sky,
Moonflower to open silver when the moon rides by;

Lilies of the valley and lupine sprays of blue,
Every friendly flower my childhood knew.
There will be a pansy bed where every velvet face,
Seems to look at me with smiling grace;

And a flagstone path with blossoms bordered gay, where I can bend
right down and make a bright bouquet; at its end a special spot
where the roses bloom,
Rose laden all the air with their sweet perfume,

Lilacs, and lots of lovely sweet-smelling things,
And birds to go skimming by with song and flash of wing; brightly
frilled hollyhocks standing high,
And a tree to mark the seasons against the sky;

Blossoms cuddled near the grass, others reaching tall,
From crocus in the early spring to asters in the fall;
A calendar of flowers to greet the unfolding year,
With red berries in the winter to give the birds cheer.

—◈—

Earth Music

There is music in the morning
As it rides the eastern sky,
Rose toned symphony of light
With the dawn star softly white.

There is music in the forest
As the wind goes rustling by,
When from every singing tree
Comes a sweet toned melody.

There is music in the city,
In its mingled sound and motion,
Rich crescendos rise and break,
Rousing chords bravura make.

There is music in the nightfall,
As the cloak of dusk descends,
Star gleams drifting from the sky
Into dream filled lullaby.

In November

A storm without, a fire within,
A day turned grey where gold had been;
And then within the darkening room,
The crackling logs to banish gloom;

You sat before the fireplace there,
The firelight shining on your hair;
And I shall always love you best,
When dusk is leading day to rest;

And you are here, alone with me,
Within this room and I can see,
While lights and shadows shift and play,
And day has turned from gold to grey,

The firelight softly gleaming there,
Upon your face, upon your hair.

Light

There are shadows in the sunlight,
Let no shadow spoil the sun;
Just keep on seeking sun bright,
Till the shadows all are done.

There are rocks upon the roadway:
Let no stones dim the sight,
To the beauty of the dawns,
Or the gleam of stars at night.

There are thorns upon the roses,
Let no thorn thrust close the eyes,
To the beauty of the blossoms,
Or the fragrance as it rise.

There is mist upon the mountain,
But the mist will fade away;
While the earth that's underfoot,
And the peaks and sky will stay.

———

Blossom Snow

In the soft May winds the blossoms blow,
Hither and thither, a fragrant snow;
The ground is petaled in pink and white,
Flower flakes flutter in sunshine bright;

A storm of fragrance in the air,
A shower of beauty, perfumed and rare,
Drifting and shifting as soft winds go,
Falling from fruit trees bending low,

Pear and apple and damson and peach,
Whirling and swirling lightly from each.
Softly falling, a petaled snow,
As gentle May winds drift and blow.

—◦◦◦—

To Hold Your Heart

Keep a song in your heart,
That shall sound sun or rain;
And weave into your life
A glad, tender refrain.

Keep a dream in your heart,
To unfurl like a flower;
Give it sun, rain and warmth
Till in beauty it tower.

Like a lamp filled with oil
With its wick ever trimmed,
Keep hope in your heart
With its flame never dimmed.

Keep faith in your heart
As you go on your way;
Ever-knowing each night
Is but prelude to day.

In your heart beauty keep,
And you ever shall know,
The beauty in all things
Realized as you go.

Keep love in your heart,
With its warmth like the sun;
To help and encourage
All the best in each one.

Keep a star in your heart
To light your soul;
To help it fulfill,
All its bright, destined goal.

Light in the Dark

My love once glowed in ecstasy,
Its radiance shining bright;
It lifted me up to the stars
And into realms of light.

But now the ecstasy is gone,
My love is mostly pain.
Strange it burns as steadily
In darkness and in rain.

Your friendship is a glowing light
To lead me out of cold and night;
The hand that has again unfurled
My banner's challenge to the world.

A song to ease the bitterest ache,
And of the world a garden make.

———

Music of the Wind

The fingers of the wind,
Make music all day long;
Gently touching leaves and grass,
Or grasping branches strong;
Turning sounds in passing by
To chorale or tender song.

Winds shake the bells on flowers,
In garden, wood and field,
While vines within their path
A rustle of music yield.

All make a mighty orchestra,
As changing winds may wield
An ever-moving baton
For percussion, reed or bow,

In variations loud and soft,
And tempo fast or slow;
The breath and fingers of the wind,
Make music as they go.

—◦◦◦—

A Rainy Day

Starting mistily at dawn,
The rain came down all day,
Dimming all the distances
And turning them to gray.

The rain began so lightly-
One looked twice to make sure,
But soon gaining force and speed,
Came with a mad downpour.

With increase of tone and tempo,
Winds joined forces to blow;
Trees seemed like ships in a tempest,
Scarce knowing which way to go.

People walking the street
Struggled nearly in vain-
Hats lost, umbrellas inside out
Between the wind and rain.

Mid-afternoon winds went down,
Wet tree branches stood secure;
Muddled birds shook out their wings,
Glad they could endure.

Rains stopped, patches of sky appeared,
A shaft of light shot out
From the hidden sun whose gleam
Gold-flecked all scattered clouds about.

While spreading wide across the sky,
A rainbow arched its glorious way,
Symbol of everlasting hope
For the end of a rainy day.

Journey

Weary with his journey through the day,
The sun continues on his downward way;
With light lower turned from gold to red,
Gladly he makes his way to bed;

Between two curved hills toward the west,
Slowly sinking as within a nest;
While twilight brings the afterglow,
And dusk her deepening covers throw

Till final dark; knowing the sun away,
The stars all hurry out to play;
The moon peeks out, no sun to fear,
And makes the sky her own both far and near,
While all of earth as it knew the day,

Finds under silver moonlight an enchanted way;
But when the night is over, come faint light of dawn,
The moon and the stars quickly hurry on,
Knowing the sun ready, from his sleep refreshed,
To make another day's journey from east to west.

Transformer

Saul traveled the Damascian Road,
Cloaked in pride with hate his goad,

So darkly deep his soul enshroud,
As sky might be in storm and cloud,

When suddenly a light so bright,
More brightly broke than light of day,

And drove him to his knees to pray,
"Why dost thou persecute me, Paul?"

Gentle the Voice and clear the call,
The evil that had been Saul's yoke,

Fell from him like a worn-out cloak.
Thus transformed within his soul,

He went as Paul, with Love his goal.

Walking

Walking makes me dream of hills,
Cascades where water spills,
A laughing brook,
Vistas with every downward look,
Framed with trees, boughs arched high,
Far hills grey-blue against the sky.

Walking takes me back again
To the days that I knew when
From a hill encircled town
I wandered pathways up and down,
From early spring till late in fall,
Hearing many a wild bird call,
Waiting till they came in sight,
Watching as they curved in flight;

Knowing many a green retreat,
Picking wildflowers at my feet fragrant air holds
Branch sweet and flowers fragrant air,
Walking takes me back once more,
Opens mountain-memoried door.

⁓

Voice of the Bell

Wedding bells are bells of gold,
Tales of romance to unfold.
Death and disaster iron bells tell,
And probe with iron into the soul.
Silver bells are dancing bells,
Songs of joy their jingle tells.

Bells of steel in triumph ring,
Tales of glory and heroes bring.
Carved brass bells with their chimes,
Tell of far places, distant times.
Church bells on the Sunday air,
Call to worship, uplift to prayer.

All man's joys and griefs may dwell,
In the voice of a bell.

Earth Ecstasy

Earth is filled with ever-changing beauty,
And I am drenched in all its loveliness;
Enchantment of the dawn, star-visioned night,
Buds unfolding, singing winds caress,
And all the endless play of shade and light;

With rainbow colors and earth music flowing
In sweeping rhythm and rich harmony,
Surging in waves upon my consciousness,
Till I am aware only of knowing—
Caught and held in this deep ecstasy,
That all of earth is living poetry.

The Root

Not any frost can more destroy
Than a season's fruit;
Though bud is nipped and leaf is lost,
The life is at the root.

Bonnets

The trees change their tops
With each changing season;
They are very much in style.
In the spring the trees wear
Easter hats of pale green lace,
Trimmed with buds and flowers;
While in summer they put on
Dark green bonnets
With bird's nests in them.

The autumn winds
Blow their hats off,
And they are left for a while
With hair of gold or of red,
Which falls out, (poor trees)
Leaving only bald branches.
But when the snows of winter come,
They all put on white wigs.

———

Straying Thoughts

Day into week, week into month,
The year went slowly by,
Helga worked with silken threads,
While on Jan's ship would ply.
He sailed the Indian ocean
Into the Arabian Sea,
Then up the Persian Gulf,
To the ports of Araby.

Helga worked and dreamed and waited,
As slow the seasons changed.
At last when came the spring,
Her marriage chest was arranged.
And as the ships sailed in,
To the dykes she would often go,
While there she watched each sail,
As into port it would blow.

Then as to her home she went,
She chose a circuitous route
That took her through the tulip fields,
Where she watched each growing shoot.
At last there came a day,
Her heart gladdened with the sight,
She saw his ship sail into port,
Her joy was at its height.

Eager and ready she waited,
Yet came he not at all.
Wondering, waiting till in the night,
Her tears began to fall.
In the morning she learned the story,
A shipmate brought the word,
He had left the ship in a Persian port,
Of him no more had they heard.

The shipmate gave her his bundle,
Rolled and snugly tied,
When opened she found a tulip,
That had been pressed and dried.

Her faith returned, her doubts swept away,
For she knew that if he lived,
He would still come back some day.
If he lived; had he just been left behind,
When they left the Persian shore?

Or had he been robbed and killed,
And would he return no more?
That year she walked the tulip fields alone,
The blossoms stood so gay and bright,
But her thoughts were of Jan...

—⟡—

Hill Hunger

I am hungry for the hills,
The hills of living green,
And I would seek the valley,
From which their slopes are seen.

Hills whose sides are brushed with gold,
When sunrise lights the day;
Where season, sun, and cloud,
Reflect each changing way.

Whose sides are warm and sweet,
As a mother's breast;
With groves of singing pine,
Where I can take my rest.

There will be winding pathways
To many hidden retreat,
And other paths that seem to climb
Till earth and heaven meet.

From mossy ways where violets bloom,
And slopes where hawthorn grows,
To pinnacles where one may view
The valley spread far below.

Until at night when stars come out,
And I would take my sleep,
The hills surround with tender care,
All night their vigil keep.

—⟨𝓌𝓈⟩—

Dawn

Dawn, like mother bird,
Stirs gently in her dark nest
To spread rose-bright wings,
While from her one golden egg,
The forthcoming day is hatched.

—∾—

The Bird of Dawn

Rising from its nest of night,
Like some great wild bird seeking flight,
The dawn lifts up rose-tinted crest,
And shakes bright feathers from its breast,
Looks on the world with a golden eye,
And lifts its wings into the sky.

—∾—

Faith of the Robin

Robin, on your ice-bound tree,
What hint of spring can you see?

Though clearly winter is not done,
You left the warmth of southern sun,
Sensing it time to fly forth,
Upon your journey to the north;

Hurrying upon the wing,
To be the first to greet the spring.
In spite of blizzard's wind and snow,
Shivering you can chirp and know

That bleak winter cannot linger,
Ruddy throated little singer.

The Task Is Ours

These are the dangerous years,
When all we love is threatened;
Our liberties and all that priceless heritage
Our fathers won, at cost of struggle
Sacrifice and blood; that which they gave us
We now must hold, to carry on
To future generations yet unborn.

The task is ours, we must not fail;
They look to us - the heroic dead,
Who gave their lives that liberty might live.
Shall we prove worthy of the gift they gave?

They look to us - all the unborn,
For as we win or fail, shall they be free or slave.
God/dess grant us valor in our task,
Open our eyes to every need, give every hand
The strength of ten
and every heart the will to win.

—⊸⊷⊷⊸—

April

April rain is silver,
April rain is gold;
April sun is playful,
April sun is bold.

April bells are tinkling
In the dewy grass;
Waking winds are sighing
Gently as they pass.

Purple bells and gold ones,
Hyacinth, daffodils,
Mingle precious perfume
As forth their fragrance spills.

Scarlet bells and blue ones,
Yellow, white and rose;
Nodding, dancing, bowing,
As the breeze gently blows.

Tulips, tall and gaudy;
Pale narcissus flower,
Weave with all the others,
A bright and fragrant bower.

April music sounding
From Robin Redbreast's throat,
Followed in the chorus,
By the bluebirds caroling note.

Happily Ever After

Love to last a lifetime long,
Happiness to weave a song;
All the things you would hold dear,
Yours to keep and really here;

A home exactly as you wish,
And in its place each chair and dish;
In cold and storm the fireplace lit,
In summer, a garden place to sit

And rest awhile when work is done,
And watch with me the setting sun;
Places to go and things to do,
Both the time-tried and the new;

Work that brings enjoyment,
And other things on which you're bent;
Books for your reading, and at your hand
The finest fruits in all the land;

And when sweet music you would hear,
Melodies to enchant your ear;
A child to love, and you to love,
And all the stars to smile above;

Achievement, rich contentment, too,
And love's fulfillment all for you.

A Changing Song

All things must pass, a flower or a star,
That which was far comes near, and near goes far;
All that we know has on it touch of doom,

Each mortal thing must go, thus making room
That newer days may come to be...
With life and love one flowing melody,

Not any of it held for over-long,
For everything is but a changing song.

—◦◦◦—

Earth Moods

I love the mad, wild moods of Earth,
The song that was sung at her fiery birth:
The lightning's flash, the thunder's roar,
The beat of the tempest's mad downpour.

I love the dash of wild winds free,
The beating and foaming of stormy sea;
Bitter snow beating against my face,
Fiery flames in their glowing grace.

I love the tender moods of Earth,
The song she sang at the flower's birth;
Spell of her power on a dew-kist rose,
Murmur of joy in the brook as it flows.

I love her rose-brushed dawns of day,
And the playful breezes gentle and gay;
The dancing fountains, the morning dew,
Fluffy clouds in skies brightly blue.

I love Earth in her moods mad and wild,
I love Earth in moods tender and mild;
I know her sorrows, her glories, her mirth,
For my pulse throbs with the heart of Earth.

—✦—

Fruit Trees

Blossoms in the springtime,
Fulfillment in the fall,
The fruit-bearing trees
Are loveliest of all.

Branches of beauty,
Fruit for harvesting;
Places in the boughs,
Where birds nest and sing.

Shadowed sunlight,
Sifting through the leaves,
With flower-fruited fragrance,
Loveliest of trees.

—∞—

Honeymoon

Days of wonder,
A month to know delight;
Moons of glory,
Star-strewn enchanted night.

Hours of romance,
A cornucopia spilled
All for our taking,
Joy now fulfilled.

—⁓—

Inspiration

Some poems unfold like flowers,
Complete in form
And color, and fragrance;

Others are like uncut jewels,
That must be shaped and polished
And placed in a setting;

While some are like flying birds,
That can only be glimpsed
As into the blue they vanish.

—⁓—

Love Theme

My heart is a song and the theme is you,
The music gives meaning to all that I do.

My heart is a star and you are its gleam,
Light out of darkness to make real the dream.

My heart is the ocean, far, deep and wide,
And caressingly close, you are the tide.

My heart is the earth and you are the sun,
Shaping the orbit where gladness is spun.

—◦◦◦—

Your Voice

Your voice is like the singing wind
That stirs the leaves upon a tree,
Until they join in their response
To weave a tender melody.

As though my heart might be a tree,
Your voice is as the wind to go,
And stir the leaves on every branch
Till the sweet song is all I know.

—◦◦◦—

Loveliness Inscribed

See beauty of the earth unfold,
Gather all the priceless gold,
Treasured scenes can be the start
Of loveliness within the heart.

Earth has music for receptive ear,
Listen well, there are songs to hear,
Cadences that become a part
Of loveliness within the heart.

Seek all good, remember to be kind,
Be true to the best you know; find
That you have inscribed a certain chart
Of loveliness within the heart.

Lupines

Blue spires,
Dew-drenched and sweet,
The lupines stood
Against the garden wall;
A bird flashed
Brightly blue above.

———

Yellow Roses

Yellow roses in a crystal bowl
Caught the ebbing light and held it,
Till they lay like clustered gold,
Within the deepening violet of the room.

———

October

There's something about October,
In its golden, leaf-blown way,
When the sun is shining through
To make a golden day;

Something that calls and beckons
And urges you along,
Stirring through your pulses
Like a lilting, vagrant song,

That has touch of gypsy magic
To carry you away,
Till it makes you a part
Of the golden, Autumn day.

Sea Call

The night is still, the stars are far,
And far is the whispering sea;

The winds are still, the night birds call,
And I hear the call of the sea;

Silent the night and distant the sea,
But I hear the surging of far-off waves,

And I see the entrances of deep sea caves,
With the ocean pouring in.

Always I hear the ocean song,
And before me sea lanes beckon and throng,

Whenever I walk on moonlit paths,
When the stars are far and the sea is far,

And the winds and the night are still.

Summer Night

Blossoms are dreaming,
Night winds sigh low;
Fragrance is drifting,
As summer winds go;
Fireflies are gleaming,
Starring the night,
Dipping and lifting,
Then suddenly bright.

Winds softly singing
Among shrubbery and trees,
The leaves are made silver
By moonlight and breeze;
A nightbird is winging
Its way in the dark,
The low branches quiver
As it may embark.

A soft music blended
In low undertone,
The frogs croak their rhetoric,
While the crickets drone
By the locusts attended
The summer night long,
The leaves to their music
Adding a song.

While shadows are dancing
As the winds caress,
On the earth strange traceries
As through the moonbeams press.
Here the moonlight glancing,
And there a soft blur,
With rise and fall of melodies
As summer voices stir.

Delighting the senses,
Soft sounds, glimmering light,
In the garden a fragrance
And flowers softly white;
While the moon dispenses
A silvery glow,
And the winds in gentle vagrance
Make music sweetly low.

—✥—

Tell Me, Wind

Wind song, wind song, what are the words that you say?
Blowing into my garden from the far away,
Do you bring a song of the sea and salt sea spray?

Or do you come from mountain peaks where the high winds blow?
Rambling down ravines with the drift of snow,
Gathering in the scent of pines and bird song as you go?

Winds, as you travel by, what do you say to me?
As you make the little leaves dance on this flowering tree,
Turning all that you may touch into new melody?

—✍—

The Real

Give me the truth,
Though bitter and hard,
To the sweetest song
Told by any bard.

Give me the storm,
To fight my way through;
Not the easy way
That is bordered with rue.

Better the effort,
And better the stress
To urge me to try -
Than fate's weakening caress.

I want more from life,
Than its pathways should please;
Give me no counterfeit,
To bring me to ease.

But life as it is,
Let me face without fear,
With all of the real
And its vision clear.

The Snowman

We built a queer white snowman,
With a hat upon his head;
He really was quite wonderful,
When that night we went to bed.

He had two eyes, a nose, a mouth,
And a stick within his hand;
He had some buttons down the front,
He was, oh, very grand.

But the sun came out next morning,
And our snowman, sturdy and tall,
Except for his buttons, stick and hat,
Just wasn't there at all.

———

Remembered Hills

Walking makes me dream of hills,
And cascades where water spills
Down into a shadowed pool,
Ringed by fern, and crystal cool.

Stones to walk across a brook,
Vistas with every downward look,
Framed with trees, boughs arched high,
Far hills grey-blue against the sky.

Walking takes me back again,
To the days that I knew when
From a hill encircled town,
I wandered pathways up and down,

From early spring till late in fall;
Listening to a wild bird call,
Waiting till it came in sight,
Watching as it curved in flight;

Knowing many a green retreat,
Picking wildflowers at my feet,
Breathing forest fragrant air,
Finding rocky ways to dare;

Or leaving footpaths to cope,
Branch by branch up a high slope.
Walking takes me back once more,
Opens a mountain-memoried door.

Abandon

Oh, life is but a dreaming,
And love is but a seeming;

So take the honey from the flower,
Dance in the sun if but for an hour,

And fling your banners to the skies,
Laughter-loving, laughter wise.

In My Poetry Room

I gather up treasures to weave on my loom,
That keeps to its task in my poetry room;
Warm threads of friendship and brightness of song,
All beauty I find as I journey along;
Warp and woof ready to weave on the loom,
Till swift shuttles dance in my poetry room.

I've woven a rug on which I can travel,
And strange, far distances unravel.....
Bright scarves of fantasy, gossamer gay,
That look ready to caper, or float away;

A shawl of rich memories to guard me from cold,
Warming and cheering when I shall grow old,
As words weave to poems on my magic loom,
Making enchantment in my poetry room.

—◦◦◦—

Moon Mist

The hushed cadence of a night in June,
The low winds sighing, the rippled croon
Of waters where stars of the sky seem strewn
And the lily fields swaying beneath the moon.

While silver arrows that are tipped with dreams,
Pierce my heart. Are they but moonbeams?
Through the birches their wonder streams
In lambent silver and nebulous gleams;

They are fairy wands in their magic power
To bring the glory of a vanished hour,
And the sweetness of a scented bower
Where the blossom of my heart had flower.

She whom I love had waited there
With the two white roses in her hair
Shedding their fragrance on the air,
While her hands were like flowers frail and fair.

She stood like a flower in her slender grace
As the moon made a halo about her face;
She wore, I remember, a gown of lace,
And I held her close in my embrace,

And I kissed her arms, her lips, her eyes,
While the very stars that sprinkled the skies
Brightened; and 'round us the rustling sighs
Of the leaves wind murmured, then paused, to rise

Till it seemed to rush and sweep and swell
In a circle about us, then hushed and fell
To a silence that throbbed with a magic spell
While all about us a glory did dwell

And the moonbeams bathed us in silver fire
That rose to the moon as an opal spire
As I whispered to her of my soul's desire
And I told her my love. Was it fairy choir

From the lily fields swaying, murmuring low
As the wind in the birches did softly blow?
Then over the moon a cloud fell slow,
And the stream of soft cadence ceased to flow

Til the only sound in the ebony night
Was a falling leaf, or a bird in flight
And the only glimmer, the fire flies' light
Or was it the lanterns of fairy-sprite?

For a magic seemed to dwell all around
And a mystic glamour about us had wound
And I held her so close that I felt the pound

Of our two hearts together chiming a song,
A paean of love, triumphant and strong,
While about us a fragrance seemed to throng
An ocean of sweetness seeming to belong

To all the flowers of all the years,
Distilled in light and love and tears;
The throbbing silence that fell on our ears
Was the very music of the spheres,

And the glamour and glow that held us fast
Was the dawn of a love that would ever last.
Then of a sudden the clouds that were massed
Over the moon, vanished and passed,

And a silver shower of moonbeam spray
Fell over the earth, in a shimmering play
Of moonlight; while a moon mist lay
Over the lily fields as they sway.

———

Morning of a Thrush Family

A brown thrush hopped upon our lawn,
I stood and watched him in the dawn,
He took a worm and up he flew,
The mother thrush was up there, too,

For when he flew into the tree,
A little nest then I could see,
Two baby thrushes were inside,
They opened up their small mouths wide,

Down went the worm, he got another,
To feed it to the first one's brother.
Their breakfast done it seemed they'd try,
To see if they could learn to fly.

For up upon a branch they hopped,
The mother thrush beside them stopped,
She spread her wings, they spread theirs too,
Then to the nearest branch she flew;

She called them but they would not come,
Their wings seemed far too cumbersome,
So back she went to try again,
Back and forth I counted ten,

But her time was not misspent,
For at last the young birds went,
She chirped her praise and let them rest,
They seemed uneasy from their nest,

But the mother bird was staunch
And flew into a farther branch;
They paused and then they thought they'd dare,
A second later they were there.

———

Music of the Wind

The fingers of the wind,
Make music all day long;
Gently touching leaves and grass,
Or grasping branches strong;
Turning sounds in passing by
To chorale or tender song.

Winds shake the bells on flowers,
In garden, wood and field,
While vines within their path
A rustle of music yield.

All make a mighty orchestra,
As changing winds may wield
An ever-moving baton
For percussion, reed or bow,
In variations loud and soft,

And tempo fast or slow;
The breath and fingers of the wind,
Make music as they go.

My Grandfather

Grandfather had a mustache and a derby hat,
And a leather armchair in which he seldom sat;
He was angular and tall like some old tree
With weathered trunk, long limbs and branches free.

He had bushy eyebrows that went up and down,
To show him in mood for a smile or a frown.
His head was completely bald on top,
But half-fringed round with a curly crop.

Fair skinned, dark haired with eyes deeply blue,
A green thumbed gardener whose front yard grew
From spring to fall in profuse bloom,
Flowers to gather for every room,

With gay bunches of blossoms to spare
For everyone who came calling there,
With the back yard a place for vegetables to grow,
Tomatoes, corn and cabbages, row on teeming row.

He took long walks with a long free stride,
But shortened his steps with me at his side.
Beside us our little black dog trotted too,
As we walked the town and the woods all through.
Grandfather carried large round peppermints along,
And often he hummed an old time song.

—⚬⚬⚬—

The Dream Is Ended

Perhaps it was not you I loved,
Not really you — for you were
But the symbol of a dream
I thought at last fulfilled.

You wore awhile this shining robe
I wove throughout the years,
Bright with ideals fine and true,
With threads of hopes and dreams

Mingled with tears that turned to jewels,
And star gleams of all that love might be,
A rich robe fit for love to wear.

The kingly garment proved
Too heavy for your little strength;
And yet — it would have been a mantle
Of strength and joy and peace,
And kept you warm against the world's alarms.

The garment too is rent, and in the dust,
While you are but a man with other men,
And look a little strange, after
The bright glory in which I viewed you;

And thus the dream is ended.

—∞—

Parallel Lives

I have lived among the hills,
And you are of the plain;
Look not on me with eyes of love,
This now you cannot gain,
Nor would I bring you pain.

For all my heart is somewhere there,
Among the hills I know,
Whose slopes know changing seasons,
Where all the wildflowers grow,
And winds in tree tops go.

Forget me now unless you can
Go with me to the hills;
I'll take you on its winding paths,
Teach you its tumbling rills,
Where crystal water spills.

We shall go through tangled woods,
And sometimes find a shadowed space,
Where the moss is velvet soft,
And ferns are like green lace,
A fairy grotto sort of place.

We shall go to hill-top heights,
Where all the valley shows below,
And winds that know the clouds,
May sometimes bend to blow
Where tallest reaching pine trees grow.

Because I'm so a part of these,
The hills a part of me,
To love me you must know the hills,
And all their beauty see,
If you'd have love of me.

⸺◈⸻

The Song of The Lark

All day long, sickle swinging from her hand,
A peasant girl had toiled over grain-covered land.
Weary she walked, her head still bent,
As slowly her homeward way she went.

When suddenly a sound was heard,
The glorious notes of a singing bird.

She stood and listened with upturned face,
Motionless, poised with unconscious grace,
Sorrow forgot, free from all care,
By the song of the lark held enraptured there.

Oh, earth is rich in lovely things,
Like the song of the lark, the flash of its wings.

———

Traveler at the Spring

Fern edged waters in a woodland spring,
Where forest birds come to drink and sing,
Through arch of silver the sun's bright lance
Turns mist to rainbow where waters dance
And tumble out with tinkling song,
To a gentler music as they flow along
Polishing pebbles smooth as glass,
Making ripples as they rise and pass.

Waters distilled from roots of flowers,
Gathering dew and sky-drenched showers,
From earth-dark source into silver pool,
Thirst quenching, sweet, and crystal cool.

Come, weary traveler, pause here awhile,
Rest from your journey of many a mile,
Leave off your hurry, toss out your care,
Breathe in the fragrance of leaf-fresh air;
Bend down beside the rock-held brink,
Fill your cup to the brim and deeply drink.

Wander

Let's follow any winding road,
That leads to anywhere;
For roads go up and roads go down,
And roads go everywhere.

It may be north, it may be south,
It may be east or west;
What matter whether it leads to the sea,
Or to a hill's green breast.

As long as there's music in the wind,
And the road's a shining curve,
As long as there's friendship in our hearts,
And beauty to observe.

There'll be adventure ahead for us,
At every turn and bend;
A glad day, a gay day,
With stars and dreams at its end.

Progress in Manhattan

There was a well-liked card shop
Where I could always find
The nicest kind of greeting,
For anyone in mind.

I hurried up the street,
Pen and stamps at hand,
And reached the spot to find
Tractors and torn up land.

There was a Five and Ten
I had not been awhile;
Was the old assistant there
Who had the friendly smile?

But where the store had been,
I found thirty floors high —
Newly made apartments,
"Ready to occupy."

———

Lesson of the Honey Bee

Draw some delight from every hour,
As bees take sweetness from the flower.

Let all experience yield its gain,
As bees transmute each pollen grain.

Find essence of all lovely things,
Nectar of sunlight, beat of wings.

Like honey—make a store of gold
To have and share against the cold.

———～∞～———

Star Taught

It was the stars that taught men's eyes,
To look upwards to the skies,
And marveling at what they saw,
Gave sense of wonder and of awe.

It was the stars whose distant light,
Penetrating space and night,
Guided travelers on their way,
As well by dark as bright of day.

It was the stars brought man to know
The universe and how stars grow,
The laws of matter and of space,
How stars and atoms keep their place.

It was the stars that stirred man's soul,
And raised him to a higher goal;
That lifted him up from the sod,
And gave an awareness of a god.

———✺———

Walking With Poetry

The rising tide of music sings
Within my heart, the day has wings
And I shall soar on melody
Within the heart of poetry,

In poetry's bright phrase and word,
Music with meaning to be heard,
Throbbing rhythms to carry far,
Echoing light from star to star.

———

Far Sea

The soul is a deep, far sea in the night,
Where waves of memory lap the distant shore
And dreams are mystic boats a-sail,
Boats that drift to port with strange cargoes,

Or float further - and further –

The cloud-veiled moon a silver mist
Of things that might have been,
While far, glittering stars flash
Rainbow fire of unattained hope.

—*w*—

Rainbow

Through your tears let rainbows shine
No matter how the heart repine
Miss not the flowers at your feet,
Nor fail to smile on those you greet.

—*w*—

Feather

I like a feather on a hat,
Placed in a certain way;
For if you have a feather
You cannot feel but gay.

Pick out a vibrant color,
And tack it with a tilt,
And everywhere you go,
You'll have a certain lilt.

There's nothing like a feather,
Insouciant and new,
Challenging and gallant,
For everything you do.

———

Summer Night

Blossoms are dreaming,
Night winds sigh low;
Fragrance is drifting,
As summer winds go;

Fireflies are gleaming,
Starring the night,
Dipping and lifting,
Then suddenly bright.

Winds softly singing
Among shrubbery and trees,
The leaves are made silver
By moonlight and breeze;

A nightbird is winging
Its way in the dark,
The low branches quiver
As it may embark.

A soft music blended
In low undertone,
The frogs croak their rhetoric,

While the crickets drone
By the locusts attended
The summer night long,
The leaves to their music

⁓

Summer Afternoon

The blue of the bellflower matches the sky,
The white summer phlox is towering high;
Petunias are pink as the flowering dawn,
Green velvet smooth is the grass of the lawn.

Dizzy with pollen the bee makes its way,
With honey collected for all of the day;
The frills of the four o'clock unfold,
While the afternoon sun spills drowsy gold.

Valley

Then on this mountain we awake
Beside a small and crystal lake
That overflows into a brook.
Come to this vantage point. Look!

The skies, a rose bowl filled with dawn,
But wait; the mists will soon be gone
That veil the valley; they disappear
Now that the morning sun shows clear,

And you may see the valley spread,
The river like a silver thread,
And fields in patches green and brown,
With every village a toy town.

You know the mountain water goes,
Tumbling down until it flows
Into a stream where waters travel,
And then with other streams unravel

Themselves into the river there,
The deep and placid waters where
All that enter keep on their way
Impelled towards the far-glimpsed bay.

Petals of Enchantment

The moon is a golden blossom,
At rest in a velvet sky,
Showering golden petals,
Earth-borne in a lullaby.

Gold petals of the moon;
Fall on poets and lovers and children,
And dispense their magical boon.

All petal-touched find a rapture,
Where the moonbeams fall,
Sense a strange and secret wonder,
Hear a far-off mystic call.

If once you follow,
A petal of the moon,
You'll find your soul is dancing
To a lilting faery tune.

You'll hear the music of the spheres,
Know a world where dreams are true;
All wonder of the universe
Will flow in light through you.

While always in your heart,
Will dwell this inner call;
An urge to ever follow
Where the golden moon petals fall.

Foot Steps

I have one restless foot,
And one that bids me stay;
One would travel any road,
That leads to far away.

One foot would follow trail,
Climb any ready plane,
Go up a waiting gangplank,
Mount steed, or bus or train.

The other foot would much prefer
To keep itself at home...
To walk upon the garden paths,
Or spade up rich brown loam,

To make ready for the planting,
Then stretch itself in the sun;
Or busy itself about the house,
To rest when the day is done.

My restless foot must carry me
To find the far away;
When curved road beckons, the distance calls,
How many miles in a day?

But never I go but my stay-at-home foot,
Soon dampens the urge to roam,
And I find that my footsteps eagerly
Are leading me back to home.

Self-Portrait

Write me in my flesh,
And give me my feet
Among the desert sands
And Porticoes on street.

Wilderness, I may go,
I'll take steps I'll leap,
A dream to fashion,
A word — and a song.

———

Prelude to Paradise

Death is an ending and a beginning,
A letting go, and new worlds winning,
Death is a ship with sunset sails,
Outward bound past earthly trails.

Death is a passport for one alone,
That leads to pathways now unknown,
Death is the passage that leads to birth,
Ascending from the dark womb of earth.

Before us the bright, flowered shores,
To bloom in glory a memory yours;
Death leads the soul to find its wings
And learn to drift from immortal springs.

Untrammeled, free, and rainbow bright,
Where life can know the speed of light.
When, seeming dead, my form
In final stillness lies;

Wear no black for me,
But only colors found
Within the rainbow.
For know that I shall go

Garlanded with stars, and clad
As morning clouds
Before the face of dawn,
Rose-tinted, glorious, free.

I shall pause briefly here
To smile on those I love,
And all the things I have found dear
Upon this rolling globe.

But wear no black and shed no tears,
For know that this closed door
Shall lead to many opened.

Know that still undimmed
My love shall shine for you,
Wherever I may be,
And all my hopes go with you.

Know that always
Upon what infinite ways I go,
I shall find beauty
And delight in it,

As you have known me do;
An ever greater beauty
And a deepening joy
To weave into my songs.

—∿—

Great Dawn Goddess

Great Dawn Goddess, bright Eros I greet thee
Fair mother of Day, I come forth to meet thee

Through dewy meadows swift I pass
Barefoot like meadow nymphs among the grass

I stoop to dip my fingers in the fragrant soil
And as the wind fingers my hair, I laugh in gladness, Earth—

Great Dawn Goddess, bright Eos I greet thee
Fair mother of Day I come forth to thee.

Dr. Dorothea Neale (1902-1999)

Internationally known poet whose poems, essays and articles on the craft of writing poetry have appeared in a variety of publications.

Founder and Director of the New York Poetry Forum (1959 to 1989), she created and directed the Forum's Saturday Workshop series and the seasonal programs of music, poetry and dance; conducted the Forum's international annual poetry contest; conceived of and managed the publication of the Forum Anthologies series:

- Perennial Promise
- Americana Anthology
- NYPF First Anthology
- Love Lyrics

Dr. Neale was the winner of numerous awards and honors including:

- International Who's Who of Poets
- International Woman of the Year (1975)
- Notable American of the Bicentennial Era
- Three-time winner of the United Poets Laureate Golden Laurel Crown
- President's Golden Medal for Poetry, Philippines
- Named International Eminent Poet by the International Poet's Academy (1987)
- Awarded Diploma D'Onore by the Internazionale Accademia (1982)

A gifted pianist, she taught Drama and Music, and also wrote, directed and produced the Saturday morning children's drama series for the Children's Play Shop, WBAL, Baltimore MD.

www.ingramcontent.com/pod-product-compliance
Lightning Source LLC
Chambersburg PA
CBHW030928090426
42737CB00007B/352